Published 1965 by P. J. Radford,
Denmead, Portsmouth
Copyright © 1965 by P. J. Radford

Designed, filmset and printed by
BAS Printers Limited, Wallop, Hampshire, England

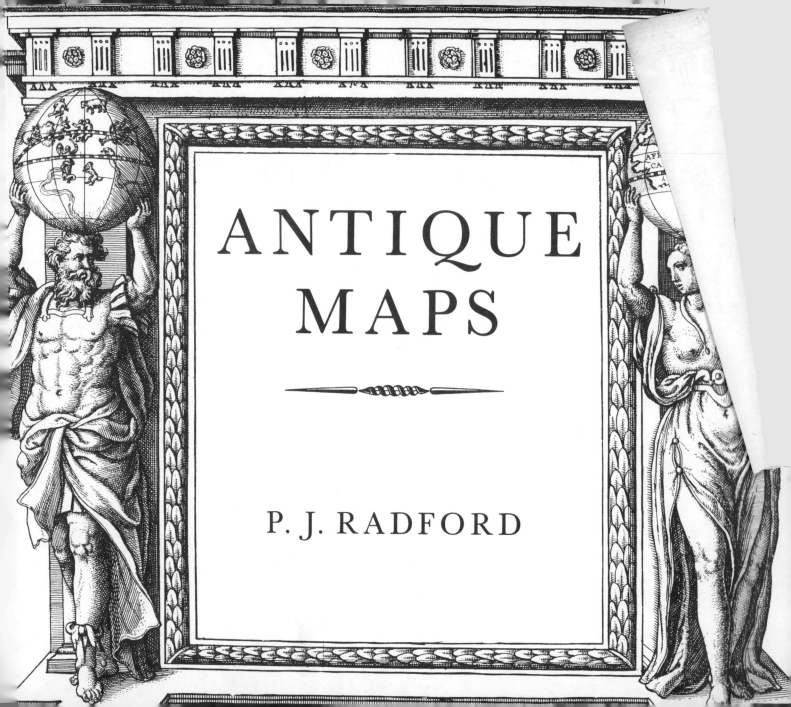

ANTIQUE
MAPS

P. J. RADFORD

Published 1965 by P. J. Radford,
Denmead, Portsmouth
Copyright © 1965 by P. J. Radford

Designed, filmset and printed by
BAS Printers Limited, Wallop, Hampshire, England

ASIA Sebastian Munster, 1545 $13\frac{1}{2} \times 10\frac{1}{2}$ inches

THERE ARE MANY people with some knowledge of old maps, but few, in my experience, know a great deal about them, and would welcome a simple, but well-illustrated guide to the subject, at a reasonable price. It is hoped therefore, that the following pages will not only be of interest but will also bring an appreciation of old maps and some understanding of the wide range that has been produced over the centuries—small and large, decorative and plain, detailed and simple, maps made for and by scholars, maps made for children, maps of countries, continents, towns, counties, states, provinces, archbishoprics, parishes, the heavens, the world—the list is very long, the range very wide.

My object in writing this little book is not to attempt a reference book or learned work on cartography—there are already some very fine books which are thoroughly recommended, and are listed at the end—but to supply a brief introduction to the subject. I feel that there is a need for a simple handbook with good illustrations as one can learn more from a good illustration than from several paragraphs of descriptive text. I have therefore arranged a series of plates that show something of various types of maps, and examples by most of the more famous cartographers. From these plates the general style of the maps of different periods will be readily seen—they are arranged chronologically so far as possible—and further, the very distinct style of each cartographer can be compared and studied. There is one thing which may be misleading if not pointed out; the maps have all been reduced for these illustrations, so note the actual size of the original which is given beneath each.

There are two outstanding points which must first be understood and they are as follows:
1. There are, of course, modern reproductions of early maps, some very good, some less so. In general it is safe to say that the only maps likely to be reproduced are the more decorative early and expensive ones, as it is obviously not worth while going to considerable expense to reproduce a map that can be bought in the original quite cheaply anywhere. Speed maps of the counties of England and Wales are well reproduced today and sell for a very few pounds, whereas an original can be considerably more, according to county. It is impossible to give a brisk *modus operandi* for detecting a modern printing from an original, but the following may help:
The paper will probably be very white, fairly thick, and smooth-faced. An old paper is sometimes white, but not brilliantly so as in a modern one. If it is lightly passed between the finger and thumb, it will feel absolutely smooth. An old paper will have a perceptible 'bite' caused by the ribbing, which was the impression left by the wire ribs of the tray with which the pulp was lifted from the water. These lines can be seen clearly when held up to the light. The watermark was the design made in wire and soldered to this tray. Some modern papers can imitate this to a certain extent. The general appearance of the maps will be 'flat' by comparison with a genuine map. Unless you have seen both together, this may be difficult to follow. The reason, of course, is that the modern map is printed from a line block, made from a photograph, which is laid on the paper; whereas the original has been printed upon a hand press under great pressure, from an engraved copper plate, and this gives it a life and depth quite lacking in the reproduction. It amounts almost to a texture.

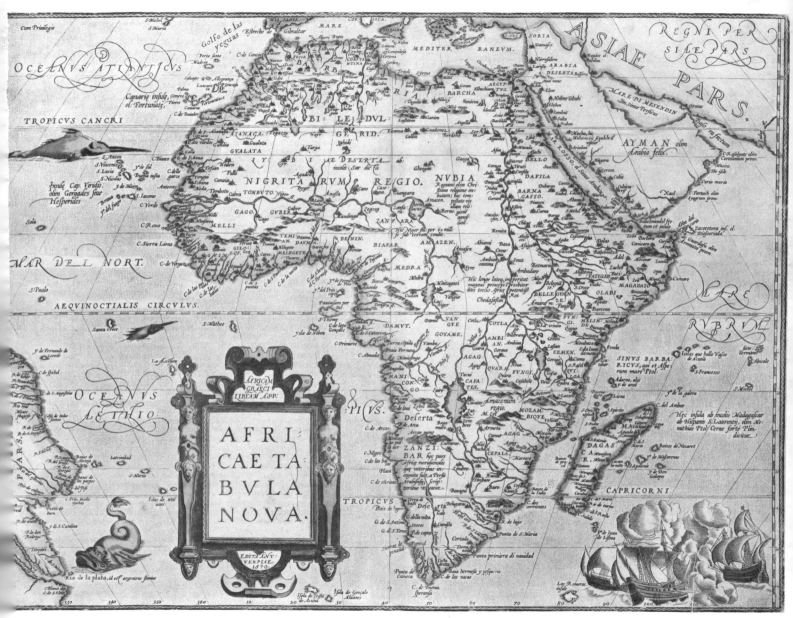

AFRICA Abraham Ortelius, 1570   19¾ × 14¾ inches

2. COLOURING

This is an important feature that has hardly been touched on in most reference books.

Some old maps were published already hand coloured. The finest are probably the maps issued by the house of Blaeu, at Amsterdam, in the middle of the seventeenth century, and they are certainly the maps you are most likely to see or purchase. Blaeu's atlases were issued plain as well, but the original colouring, although within the limits of a definite style, varies with the individual groups of colourists, and sometimes, one feels, with the price charged. Sometimes the colours are laid on simply, with modest shading, whilst at the other end of the scale they are painted in great variety, with as many as four different tints of the same colour for shading, and enriched with liquid gold. One common factor runs through all the styles—whatever Blaeu produced, the design, execution and colouring was inspired by superb taste. Blaeu maps are the very quintessence of all that is best in the artistic expression of the period, applied to cartography.

A century earlier, Saxton maps of the counties were published, many sets being superbly coloured and often enriched with gold leaf. One suspects that colouring was done to order, however, as atlases were seldom issued coloured in this country. It was usual for the purchaser of an atlas to take it to a map colourist and to have the work done to his express order. This has been the case with maps by Speed, Kip, Hole, Morden and Blome. It was not until the late eighteenth century that atlases were sold ready coloured in any quantity.

There is no doubt that many people coloured their own (this is, unhappily, all too evident with some of our native efforts), as books of general instruction for young gentlemen have details, not only of how to colour, but how to make up the colours in the first place. These instructions were issued and re-issued through the eighteenth and into the nineteenth centuries.

Here is one version from a book of 1800:
'For colouring maps, an amusement both extremely agreeable and of great advantage, besides the colours, gum water and tartar ley are principally requisite.

Gum Water may be made in this proportion. Three ounces of whitest and clearest gum arabic, beat small, may be dissolved in a pint of fair spring water: shake it two or three times a day very well. If there is any foulness in it, strain it through a rag into a clean earthen dish, and then bottle it for use. It should be made fresh every two months; therefore small quantities are best at once.

Tartar Ley is made in this manner. Wrap about two ounces of the best white tartar very tight in half a sheet of brown cap paper, thoroughly wet; put it into a clear fire of wood or sea coal, to remain till it is red hot, when it must be taken out with the tongs, and immediately put in a pint of water. Rub it well to pieces with your fingers, and put all into a long narrow glass; in a day or two the clear ley may be decanted off, and, when put into a clean glass, kept for use.

COLOURS of a superior brightness and lustre are made as follows, peculiarly calculated for improving and embellishing maps.

A COPPER GREEN is thus made. Take a quantity of the best French verdigris, which beat into a fine powder, with about one-fifth of cream of tartar, avoiding the fumes of verdigris by stuffing the nose, and holding some fine linen in the mouth. Mix the powders in about five or six times their weight of water, which boil away in an earthen pipkin to half; and when cold, strain it, putting the liquor into a glass, which stop up, and let it stand to settle till the liquor is very clear. If it should not be deep enough, diminish it by a gentle heat over a few

LANCASHIRE Christopher Saxton, 1577   19 × 15½ inches

coals, and try its strength by a slip of white paper. But it should not shine too much; this will sometimes make it necessary to boil it anew with some more verdigris, so as to become a transparent, deep willow green. This colour will keep many years, if close corked. A little quantity may be made in a small pot or cup over a few hot embers.

A STONE-COLOUR is made by boiling an ounce of the best myrrh, in powder, in a pint of the tartar ley, till it is dissolved. A short time will do it; pour off the clear liquor, when settled, for use, keeping it close stopped. It will never decay: boil away the liquor to make it deeper, or add water to make it fainter.

A CRIMSON COLOUR may be made with about 30 or 40 grains of good cochineal, bruised to fine powder in a gally pot, adding as many drops of tartar ley as will just wet it, and force the colour. Put half a spoonful of water to it immediately, or more, if it is too deep; you will have a delicate PURPLE COLOUR or Tincture. Scrape a very little allum into the tincture, and it will change into a delicate crimson; it should be used soon, as it decays with keeping.

For a BLUE, grind indigo very fine on a stone, with a little tartar ley; and when like a thick syrup, add gum water to it, and keep it in a glass close stopped. When you use it, stir it up from the bottom.

Gamboge makes the best YELLOW, in a lump of which make a hole with a penknife to put in some water; stir it well with a pencil, to make a faint or deeper yellow as you require. Pour it into a gally pot, and temper more till you have enough.

Red lead and orpiment may be had at the shops very finely ground, which temper with gum water for use. Blue bice needs only to be tempered in the same manner. Ultramarine, though dear, will go a great way with care, and may be mixed with a little gum water in a very small gally pot.

Carmine is a very dear colour, but may be tempered to various degrees of crimson with gum water, and should be used with care. Vermillion is a beautiful scarlet, if so tempered; but it shows much brighter when dry, if glazed over with some thick gum water, in proportion of two ounces of gum arabic to half a pint of water or less.

Burned umber, for some uses, if ground very fine, and thick as possible, and then tempered with gum water to a proper thickness, makes a good transparent colour.

A pleasant GRASS GREEN is made by taking a lump of gamboge (as for yellow) and mixing it in some copper green; by stirring it with a pencil, it will change from a willow to grass green, and will be deeper or lighter, according to the time you stir it.

TO COLOUR THE MAPS

The divisions in a map which distinguish one kingdom from another, or one country from another, are known by certain lines or rows of pricks, or points of several sizes and shapes, agreeable to the divisions they are to denote. In a map of Spain and Portugal, for instance, the two kingdoms are separated by a row of large points or pricks, and the several provinces (such as we call shires in England) are distinguished by lines or lesser points. Then, to colour Portugal, cover the hills within the large pricked line with very thin tincture of myrrh, or tincture of Jesuit's bark; and, where there are woods, dab every tree with the point of a very fine pencil dipped in grass green, made with gamboge and copper green. In dipping your pencil, stroke it against the side of the pot or glass where your colour is, to prevent its dropping. The principal cities and towns may be marked with another pencil dipped in red lead, thinly tempered with gum water, that the eye may readily perceive them.

Penõn de Velez

Barbariæ Pars

SEPTENTRIO

HISPANIAE PARS

OCEANUS

MARIS MEDITERRANEI PARS

ATLANTICUS

INSULÆ FORTUNATÆ Ptolemæo,
at nunc CANARIÆ INSULÆ ob ingentes
canes, quorum ibi magna copia à Portugalensibᵘ inventa.

REGNVM
MAROCHI

DARA REG.

SEGELMESSE

ZAHARA alys

ZANHAGA

MERIDIES

FESSÆ et
MAROCCHI
REGNA.

Scala
Hispanicarum Leucarum

Milliaria Germanica communia

MOROCCO Gerard Mercator, 1595   19 × 14 inches

To trace out the bounds of the provinces, take another pencil dipped in copper green, which move along the inside of the pricked lines, laying it evenly on. The next province may be coloured in like manner with gamboge, the next with the crimson tincture of cochineal, the next with red lead, the next with grass green, and then any of the former colours. Observe, that no two provinces must in any part join with the same colour: and that where the provinces join, the second colour must not be laid on before the first be dry. The colours may be lightened off, or made fainter, when nearly dry, by wetting a clean pencil in water, gently squeezing it out, and going round with it on the inside of the coloured line.

Note, that where any towns, trees, hills, etc., have been coloured before the bounds are marked out, those places must continue, and not be coloured again with any other tincture or colour. Landscapes may be coloured according to nature, as may all other devices or figures which are introduced to set off and embellish maps. Our limits will not allow us to be more particular; and therefore we shall only add in general, that the water and the bottoms of ships are to be tinged with thin indigo, the hull with umber, the sails with tincture of myrrh, and the flags with vermillion or blue bice, according to their respective colours. The smoke of the guns, where necessary, be done with very thin bice; and lastly, the border or margin of the map may be coloured either with yellow, red, crimson, or any other lively colour at pleasure.'

It will be noted that the green is made from verdigris. This had an unfortunate effect on the map as it slowly rotted the paper upon which it was painted, especially if exposed to the light much, so that the paper became brittle along the boundary with the result that the whole section so outlined falls out of the map. If dealt with in time by strengthening the back with old paper, this risk is eliminated.

There are a few broad points in connection with the style of colouring at various periods which might be of interest; they are as follows:

Sixteenth to early seventeenth centuries. Outline colouring on map area, often faded off at one side, but some areas will be completely washed in, often in green. Boundary lines often wide.

Early seventeenth to late eighteenth centuries. Outlines only on boundaries. No fading off.

Late eighteenth to mid nineteenth centuries. Outline but with most areas completely washed in with a very pale, smooth tint of the boundary colour. These very smooth washes were aided by the addition of ox-gall to the gum-water. Some colourists added sugar if the paper tended to be greasy. Ear wax was also prescribed! Very narrow pen-drawn boundary lines.

Now most of the colouring you will see on maps will be quite modern, and here one must be careful, as many fine maps have been quite ruined by careless application, appalling colours (often straight from the jar of poster colour) and worst of all, the maps have not been sized. This last point is important because if the map has first been sized, and the colouring is not up to standard, it can mostly be washed off without harming the map; whereas an unsized map cannot have any colour removed, for it will have sunk right into the paper. Such bad workmanship can sometimes be minimised by sizing over the colour, and recolouring with colours carefully mixed to complement the existing colour on the map, so that the garish or crude tint is mellowed and partially neutralised. This is expert work, and it is usually better not to buy such a map.

Colouring need not be mellow and 'antique' in appearance—it should be a blend of pleasant *and*

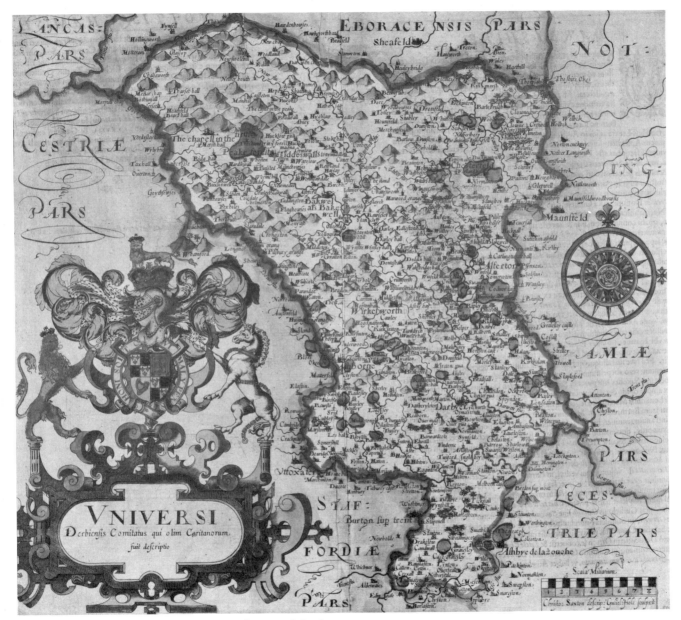

DERBYSHIRE William Hole, 1607   12¼ × 11⅛ inches

suitable shades, the bright colours being set off by more subtle tints. There should be some sort of colour balance based on the primaries—red, yellow and blue, but this cannot apply in every case. And it should be carefully applied.

I stress this aspect of the appreciation of old maps because there is so much bad work about—and some very fine work. You will probably pay as much for a garish example as for a professionally-coloured map, so you might as well select the best at the start.

Before leaving the subject of colouring, it might be as well to have a look at the question of framing, as this can also make or mar with a vengeance.

The best frame is undoubtedly one of the black and gilt Hogarth mouldings. This particular type shows the map off to better advantage than any. There are many types of Hogarth, imported from Scandinavia, Belgium and Italy, whilst some are made in this country. Quality varies considerably, but if you want to pay a valuable map the supreme compliment, you can obtain a hand-carved Hogarth moulding which comes from Italy.

Do not have a moulding which is too narrow for the size of the map. A map of 20 × 15 inches or larger by one of the earlier, heavier, engravers (Speed for instance) needs not less than $\frac{3}{4}$ inch moulding, whereas a map of this size of lighter engraving (Cary) can be quite effective in $\frac{1}{2}$ inch, but of course the narrower the moulding and the larger the map, the weaker the frame at the corners in relation to the weight of glass.

THE MAKERS OF PRINTED MAPS IN APPROXIMATE CHRONOLOGICAL ORDER OF THEIR PRINCIPAL PRODUCTIONS.

This list includes some examples that are difficult to acquire, but excludes the excessively rare. The cartographers marked with an asterisk produced maps of individual counties in the British Isles. Most of the others produced maps of the British Isles as a whole, or parts thereof.

SEBASTIAN MUNSTER. Born at Hessen in 1489 he worked from the 1530's having completed his education at Heidelburg and Tübingen. His maps are printed from woodblocks, and one can obtain small maps by him at very reasonable rates, considering their antiquity. His larger maps are more coveted, especially the fine Americas, Africa and World maps; they were the first separate maps of continents, but there are those by him of many other parts. Some of the earlier issues have fine woodcut borders upon the verso.

ABRAHAM ORTELIUS. A famous name and justly so, for his maps are superb works of art: the result of scholarship and a finely cultivated artistic sense. He was born at Antwerp on April 4th 1527 and after an extensive education, he and his sister commenced in business selling, and sometimes colouring, maps. In 1570 he published his great collection of maps, the first real atlas as we understand the term today. Many subsequent issues were published and printed by the Plantin Press (which handled and produced work of very fine quality) the last being in 1612. The text on the back of the maps was in a number of languages—Latin, German, Spanish, Dutch, French and, in 1606, English. A delightful series of miniature maps was produced by him and published from 1576. He died on June 28th 1598.

*CHRISTOPHER SAXTON, born in Yorkshire, probably at Tingley, near Leeds about the year 1542. After completing his education at Cambridge, he came to London and joined the household of

THE SABRINIAN SEA

THE FRENCH SEA

DEVON AND CORNWALL William Hole for Michael Drayton, 1612 $12\frac{3}{4} \times 9\frac{1}{2}$ inches

Queen Elizabeth's Master of the Court of Requests and Surveyor of the Court of Wards and Liveries, Thomas Seckford. Evidently realising that Saxton had considerable talent as a surveyor, Seckford encouraged him to survey the counties of England and Wales, paying his expenses and obtaining the authority for the work of no less a person than Queen Elizabeth. Armed with this authority, he could ascend any tower or hill he needed for surveying purposes and eventually compiled a set of maps for which the finest engravers, mostly from the Low Countries, were engaged—Augustine Ryther, Remigius Hogenburg, Leonard Terwoort. These maps, the first ever issued of the counties, were a magnificent result of a truly stupendous effort; and the final engraving on copper, executed between 1574 and 1579 fully justified the undertaking. The maps have a restrained exuberance in their decoration; lettering of great beauty for the place names; and were coloured, some being heightened with gold. Each bears the Royal Arms of Elizabeth, and the Arms of Seckford. The earliest impressions are in all probability those with the 'grapes' watermark —a lozenge of small circles; slightly later issues are those bearing the crossed arrows watermark. These maps of Elizabethan England are always rising in price, but are well worth having, whatever the county. They were reprinted in 1645 and in an altered form in 1689 and 1693, and then in the eighteenth century in 1720 and 1749. Saxton died some time after 1606.

GERARD MERCATOR. The first map-maker to give a systematic collection of maps the name 'Atlas'. Born in Rupelmonde on March 5th 1512, he was responsible for producing a set of exceedingly fine maps, with much of the same attention to detail and delight in fine design that characterised the maps of Ortelius. Mercator's atlas was published in three parts between 1585 and 1595, by which year he had died, but his sons and grandsons carried on the cartographical tradition with later issues of his works, adding maps of their own. Again the text on the back was issued in a number of languages. He included maps of individual countries but produced some fine and interesting maps of groups of counties. In 1606 Jodocus Hondius bought the plates and re-issued them in an extended atlas. Later still John Jansson joined him, and more maps were added until eventually he took over the whole business.

*JOHN NORDEN is something of a tragedy in British topography. He was born in 1548, possibly in Somerset, and set out to produce a set of maps of the counties from his own surveys, like Saxton, but being unable to obtain a patron to finance him, he completed but a few surveys and succeeded so far as is known, in producing maps of only Middlesex (1593), Surrey (1594), Sussex (1595), Hampshire (1595), Hertfordshire (1598), and probably Kent, although no maps are known. These are all very rare indeed—only one copy of the Sussex map is known, and that is in the library of the Royal Geographical Society. I include Norden's name in these pages, however, as his surveys were used by others (see W. Hole and W. Kip) and the known maps were reissued in the early eighteenth century. These are the specimens one is most likely to obtain. Norden died about 1625.

*The ANONYMOUS MAP-MAKER. Apparently another abortive attempt at a set of county maps was commenced in 1602–1603. They are fairly simple in style, mainly based on Saxton and Norden, but some have many more place names added. They are mostly known from the later issues of Stent and

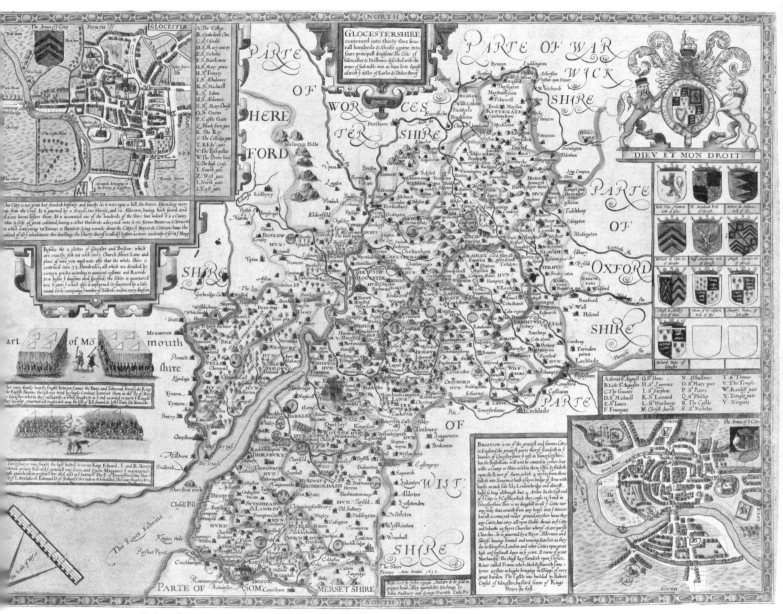

GLOUCESTERSHIRE John Speed, 1610–11   20 × 15 inches

Overton, produced in the late seventeenth and early eighteenth centuries. The counties known are as follows:—Leicester and Rutland, Norfolk, Cheshire, Essex, Warwick, Suffolk, Worcs, Surrey, Lancs, Staffs, Northants and Herts. All are rare. They were almost certainly engraved by Jodocus Hondius, from originals prepared by William Smith. These facts have only come to light in recent years as a result of research by Mr. R. V. Tooley, who discovered some of the original drafts; and of Mr. R. A. Skelton of the Map Room, British Museum.

*WILLIAM HOLE. An early and fine English engraver who worked in London from about 1600 to 1646. He was the first in this country to engrave music upon copper plates. He produced a number of fine county maps, working with William Kip. They took Saxton's and, where possible, Norden's surveys as their basis, and composed entirely original maps from them. Hole also engraved the strange maps for Michael Drayton's poem 'Poly-Olbion' issued in 1612 and 1622 which are described under Drayton's name. Little is known of Hole's life. His colleague on the 1607 county maps was

*WILLIAM KIP who worked between approximately 1598 and 1635, and tended to engrave a slightly less decorative map, but they are still superb works. Both Kip and Hole were producers of work of a very high standard and their place names are beautifully done. The set of maps of the English and Welsh counties which they produced, went through three issues, and each can be clearly distinguished by an amateur if he will bear the following simple points in mind:—The first issue, produced in 1607 has Latin text on the back; the second issue 1610 has a plain back; the third issue, 1637 and the one most usually seen, has a plain back

and a numeral engraved in the bottom left-hand corner of most counties. There are a few exceptions to this, including Bucks, Cheshire, Hunts, Ireland, Salop, Scotland, East Riding and North Riding of Yorkshire, and the following Welsh counties: Brecon, Denbigh, Flint, Merioneth, Pembroke and Radnor, these maps are all without the numeral. Brecon was completely replaced in 1637 by an almost identical map engraved by Robert Vaughan.

*PIETER VAN DEN KEERE. A Dutch engraver, bookseller, and artist, who worked between about 1590 and 1620, much of the time in England, probably with Jodocus Hondius (who engraved many fine maps, including a number of Speed's). He engraved maps of many different types, but his name is principally connected with the beautiful set of miniature maps he began producing in Amsterdam in 1599, published by Blaeu in 1617— the maps were based on Saxton's maps inasmuch as he grouped counties together where Saxton had done so, although naturally, but a fraction of the place names could be inserted. From 1620 the plates were reprinted by John Speed, with the grouped counties (Kent, Sussex, Surrey and Middlesex etc.) engraved as a separate map for each county, Keere almost certainly doing the engraving. It is because Speed published the maps from 1620–1676, with additions—parts of the world were added to the collection from 1627—that they are so commonly known as 'miniature Speeds.'

*JOHN SPEED. Probably the most widely known name in early county maps, and the most sought after. Speed was born at Farndon, Cheshire, in 1552. His father was a tailor; like him, John Speed followed the same trade for a number of years, and in 1580 was admitted to the Merchant Taylors Company. He married two years later, and

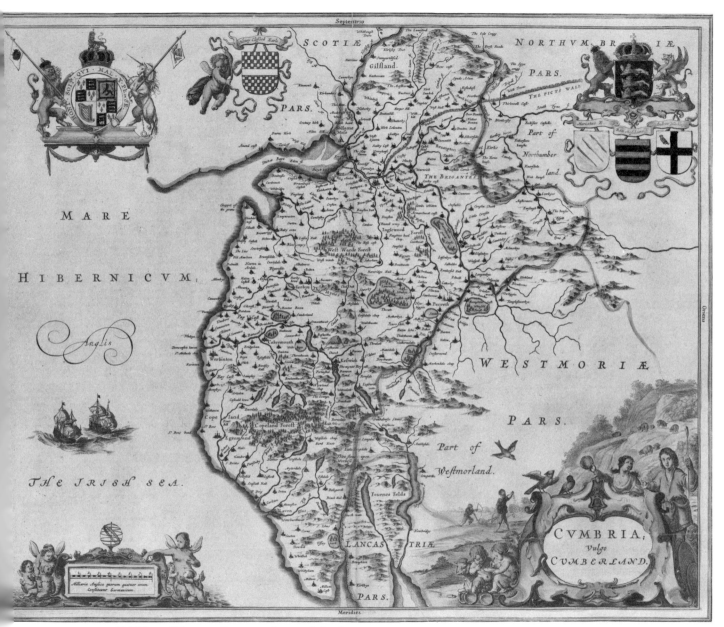

CUMBERLAND William Blaeu, 1645   19⅝ × 16 inches

probably lived at Moorfields, studying history when he could and becoming a historian of note. He began his series of magnificent county maps, introducing much heraldry, town plans, and ornamentation which includes figures, ships and sea monsters, as well as small battle scenes in blank areas outside the county boundary. His sources were the best he could obtain—Saxton, Norden, the Anonymous maps and many others. He is also notable for two very unusual features. He indicated his sources on the map, and he revised the various names, adding details and place names where necessary. Furthermore, the text on the back of the map is always complete, whereas the text on other maps of the seventeeth century is invariably only part of the whole; each of Speed's maps has a description and history of the county on one half, and a list of towns and villages on the other half. The maps were issued and reissued to an extent that has only recently been fully realised, but those quite likely to be seen are as follows:

1611 The first and without doubt the finest. On thick paper and a very rich dark impression, usually with good top and bottom margins.

1615 A very good early issue.

1616 The quite rare Latin issue, the text on the back being in that language.

1627–1631 Another good issue. It was the first to include a set of maps of various parts of the world.

1646 An unusual issue, but there are maps from it to be found. The last of the 'early' Speeds, i.e., those bearing the names of the original publishers, Sudbury and Humble of Pope's Head Alley, London (still existing between Cornhill and Lombard Street).

1662 Usually nicely printed and mostly bearing the imprint of Roger Rea as publisher.

1676 A frequently seen issue. The plates were now getting very worn, and the impressions are pale; often the hatching on the sea does not come out at all; the paper varies from thick to thin. The maps were published by Bassett and Chiswell, and bear their imprint. This issue had the maps of parts of the world augmented by the addition of maps of New England and New York, Virginia and Maryland, Carolina, Jamaica and Barbados, Palestine, Russia and the East Indies. Still later issues were to come out.

John Seller's of 1680 is a plain-backed and quite scarce one. Henry Overton's of 1710, 1713 and 1743 is a plain-backed issue, often with early colouring on the boundaries, and mostly with his imprint added. Dicey's issue of 1770 is quite rare.

Although the earlier issues are by far the best in appearance, there is no doubt that the plates bore up surprisingly well in view of the fact that edition after edition was being printed from them for over a century and a half—they were repaired, altered, renewed, re-engraved, but the same basic Speed map is still with us in the eighteenth century as it was throughout the seventeenth. Not the least interesting feature of Speed's county maps are the miniature town plans on most of the maps with their 'Scale of Pases' and tiny figures on horseback, or ploughing, in the fields outside the towns. His maps of the World, Africa, Europe and other parts are mostly very fine, with their views of cities in a border at the top and figures standing in niches down the sides.

*MICHAEL DRAYTON, Poet. His only work to interest us here is the publication of his 'Poly-Olbion,' issued in two parts in 1612 and in 1622. This issue was illustrated by decidedly strange maps which show practically no place names, but indicate the principal towns by crowned figures, usually female, whilst hills or mountains are shown, usually surmounted by a seated shepherd. The more

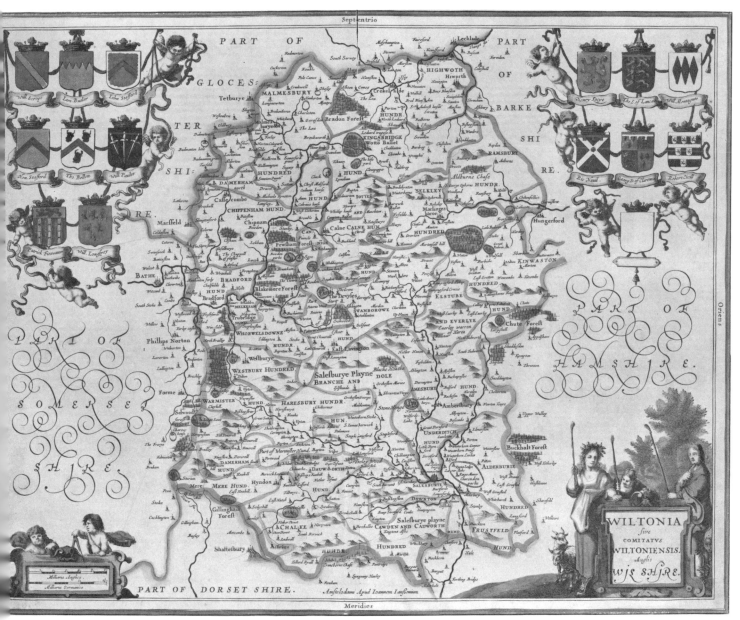

WILTSHIRE John Jansson, 1646   19½ × 15½ inches

famous forests are often shown, usually with a Diana in charge, whilst each river sprouts a small nude nymph. There are no boundaries, and some counties are grouped together. The maps have an undeniable fascination, and are decorative in an arcadian and masque-like way. They were engraved by William Hole.

JOHN BILL, 1626 published a rare set of miniature maps, very similar in style to those of Keere, but if anything, slightly more attractive.

*WILLIAM (WILLEM) BLAEU was born at Alkmaar in 1571. He died on October 21st, 1638 at Amsterdam. His son, Joan Willem was born at Amsterdam in 1596, and there was a second son, Cornelis. They died in 1673 and 1642 respectively. The Blaeu's produced the finest set of maps of the seventeenth century. Their general quality of design, execution, paper and colouring were of the best. They brought out a set of superb county maps, after Speed, utilising the same heraldry, but composed the whole into a totally different type of map. They also produced the earliest printed maps of the counties and provinces of Scotland, a fine and unusually interesting set of maps which were engraved from the late sixteenth century surveys of Timothy Pont, a minister. Several were engraved from the maps of the editor of Pont's surveys, Robert Gordon of Straloch.

*JOHN (JAN) JANSSON was born at Arnhem in 1596, and produced a fine and decorative set of maps (which included the English and Welsh counties) often handsomely coloured. This was published in various languages and many editions between 1638 and 1657. He died at Amsterdam in 1664. The maps were, however, published again by Valk and Schenk towards the end of the seventeenth century, in about 1683. Jansson's maps, though fine, are in very many cases slavishly copied from works of Blaeu.

MATTHEW SIMONS, 1636. A most unusual set of tiny 'thumb-nail' maps occupying a triangular corner of a page of distance-scales (on the same principal as still employed in the motoring organisations' handbooks), the object being a map and distance table of each county for the benefit of the traveller. Other editions were published by Thomas Jenner in 1643 and 1668.

NIKOLAUS VISSCHER. There were several, each succeeding the other throughout the seventeenth century. Between them they produced some very fine maps, full of detail, with superb engraving and beautifully executed cartouches with figures and shields.

CAROL ALLARD was another map-maker of about this period which extends into the eighteenth century. His maps are very similar in style to those of the Visschers.

FREDERICK DE WIT also produced some magnificent maps from about 1670 in the same style with many place names and fine cartouches. A large number were reissues of maps by Jansson, Allard and others.

JOHN OGILBY. Born at Edinburgh in 1600 and obviously a colourful character from that year! Before he died at the age of 76 he had been the owner of a theatre, a bookseller, a dancing master, a translator of the classics, a printer and a famous map-maker. In 1641 he lost his money in the Irish Rebellion, and his whole livelihood again in the Fire of London. He produced some fine books after Arnold Montan dealing with the Americas, Africa

18

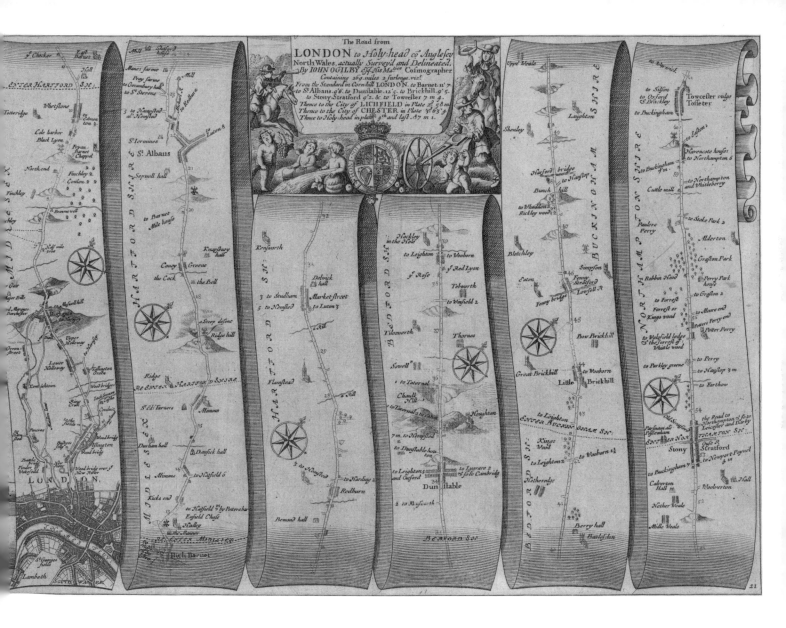

LONDON TO TOWCESTER John Ogilby, 1675   17 × 12¼ inches

and Asia, using his plates in most cases, but is most famous for his very fine series of strip road-maps which were such an innovation when published in 1675. Each road was mapped with great skill, being actually measured with a 'waywiser'. The maps of the roads from York to Scarborough; Oxford to Cambridge; London to Towcester; and London to Oxford have cartouches which show this instrument being used. The maps are most ingenious, giving all one should know in a simple form. Starting from the bottom left-hand corner each strip is read upwards. The hills one ascends are shown as usual, as a mound, but when the road descends, the hill is shown inverted. The changes of direction are shown by inserting a second compass with a different bearing into the strip after a dividing line across the map. Items of interest as well as practical use are shown —'a smith's shop', 'ye worst way . . .'. They were the first maps to adopt the present standard mile. The length of the mile varied in different parts of the country. (Robert Morden's maps had three different scales on each map.) These road maps were copied in miniature without decoration, by both Thomas Gardner, and also by John Senex, in 1719. Gardner's were a little larger than those of Senex. The following year Emanuel Bowen and Thomas Owen brought out their 'Britannia Depicta' a beautiful little work, each page being wholly engraved by Bowen. Unfortunately the books have been broken up for the series of miniature county maps. Any of the pages are attractive and of considerable interest, as the road maps are enlivened with coats-of-arms, notes and similar detail.

*RICHARD BLOME. A poor engraver and an unashamed plagiarist but with an undeniable decorative sense. Although crudely engraved many of his maps have great antique charm, with their cartouches, arms, or other features. He published maps of parts of the world at the end of the seventeenth century and his set of county maps was printed in 1673; a delightful miniature series came out in 1671, again in 1681 and with a number of the maps in altered form in 1715; this was reprinted several times during the following twenty years. It is interesting to know that Blome's prospectus, sent out to possible subscribers offered the printing of the subscriber's name, title, seat and coat-of-arms at the front of the 'Britannia' of 1673 for the payment of £1. But for £4 he could have the map of his choice dedicated to him and with his coat-of-arms. A prospectus in my possession bears the receipt in Blome's hand for the sum of £3 14s. 6d. 'for one of my vols of Britannia with ye Dedication of Breck-nockshire which with ye former fifteen shills pd when he subscribed makes four pounds nine shill and sixpence owing to ye sd. proposal' and is signed by him.

*ROBERT MORDEN. Map-maker, bookseller and publisher in the latter half of the seventeenth century and first half of the eighteenth. He had premises in Cornhill from 1688 to 1703 where he sold books and maps under the sign of Atlas. A number of maps of various parts of the world by him may be met with, many of small size which were issued from 1688, but he is best known for his fine series of county maps first published in 1695, and in later issues of 1722, 1753 and 1772. Each map is clearly engraved, with plenty of place names, and embellished with a cartouche. These maps are the most reasonably priced of all the larger seventeenth century county maps. The fact that there are a lot about in no way detracts from their general excellence. A rule-of-thumb guide to the issues (to which, of course, there are exceptions) is as follows: First 1695—Usually rather thin paper, good black

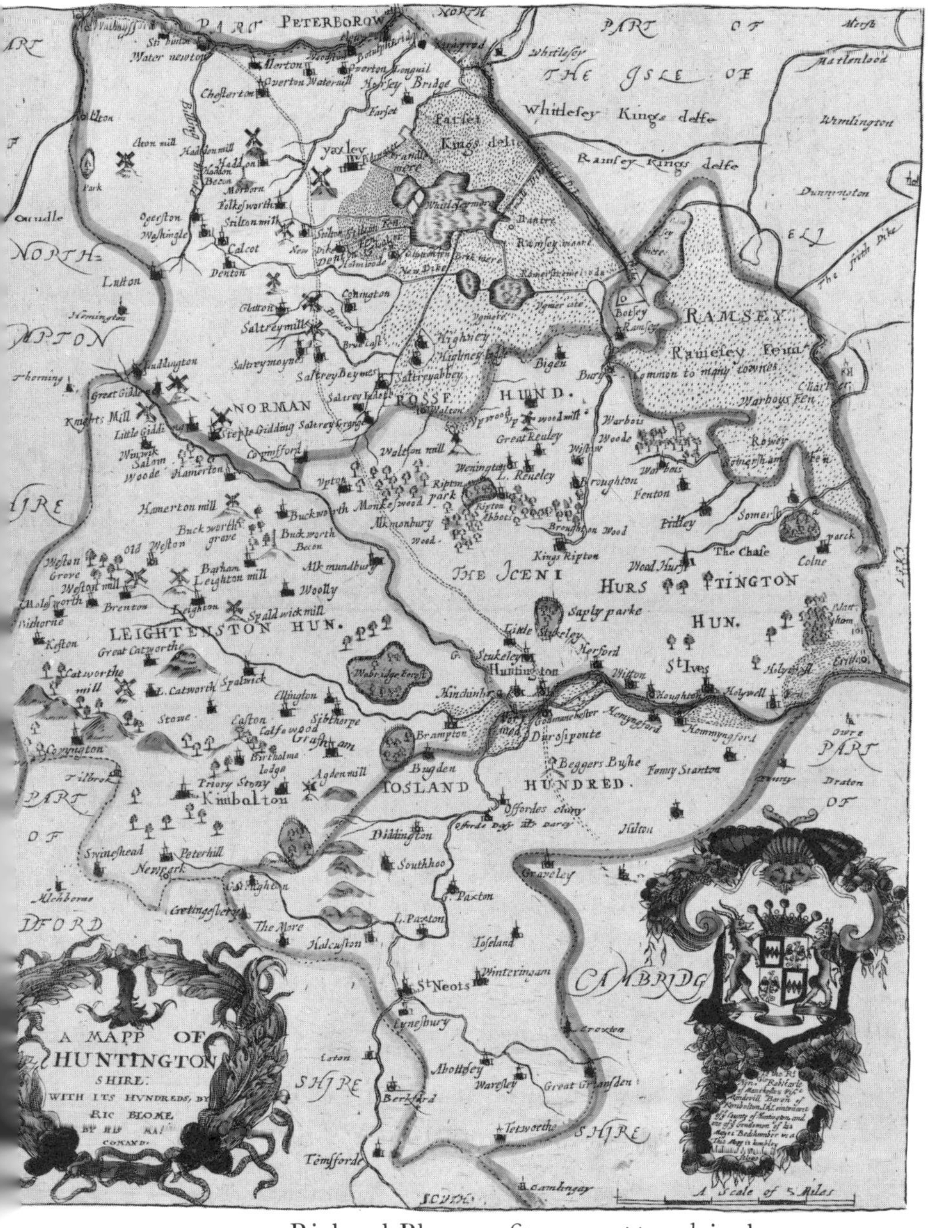
A MAPP OF HUNTINGTON SHIRE: WITH ITS HVNDREDS, BY RIC BLOME BY HIS MAI COMAND
PART OF PETERBOROW
THE ISLE OF
ELY
RAMSEY
NORMAN
HUND.
LEIGHTENSTON HUN.
THE ICENI
HURSTINGTON HUN.
TOSLAND HUNDRED.
CAMBRIDG SHIRE
A Scale of 5 Miles

HUNTINGDONSHIRE Richard Blome, 1673 10 × 12½ inches

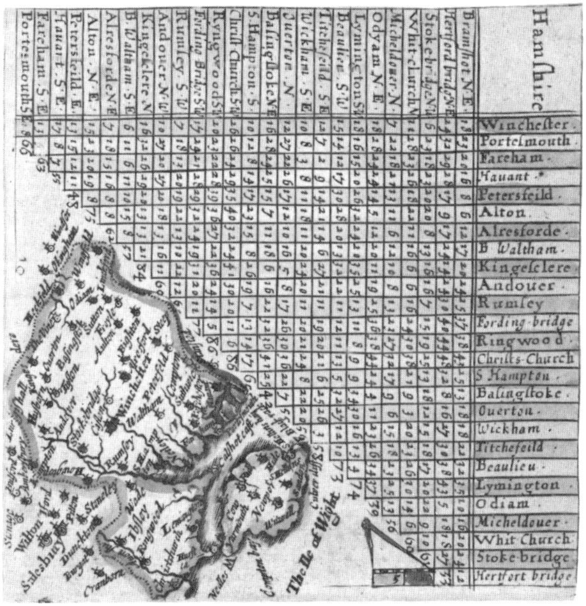
Hamshire
Winchester
Portesmouth
Fareham
Hauant
Petersfeild
Alton
Alresforde
B Waltham
Kingsclere
Andouer
Rumsey
Fording bridge
Ringwood
Christs Church
S Hampton
Balingstoke
Ouerton
Wickham
Titchefeild
Beaulieu
Lymington
Odiam
Micheldouer
Whit Church
Stoke bridge
Hertfort bridge
The Ile of Wight

HAMPSHIRE Matthew Simons, 1636
4⅛ × 4⅛ inches

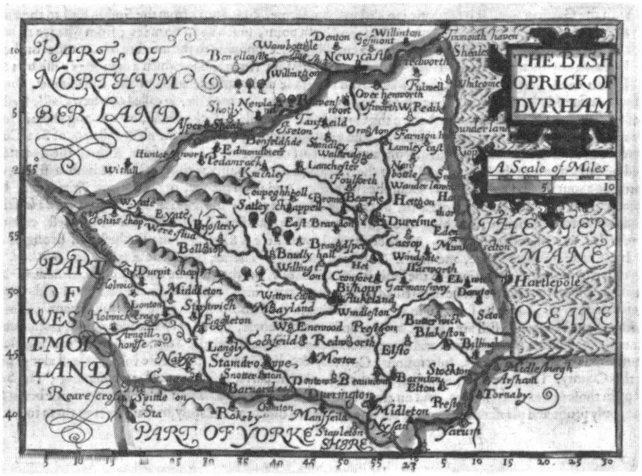
THE BISHOPRICK OF DVRHAM
PART OF NORTHVMBERLAND
PART OF WESTMORLAND
PART OF YORKE SHIRE
THE GERMANE OCEANE
A Scale of Miles
Newcastle
Durefme
Hartlepole

DURHAM John Bill, 1626
4¾ × 3¼ inches

DORSET Robert Morden, 1695   16½ × 14¼ inches

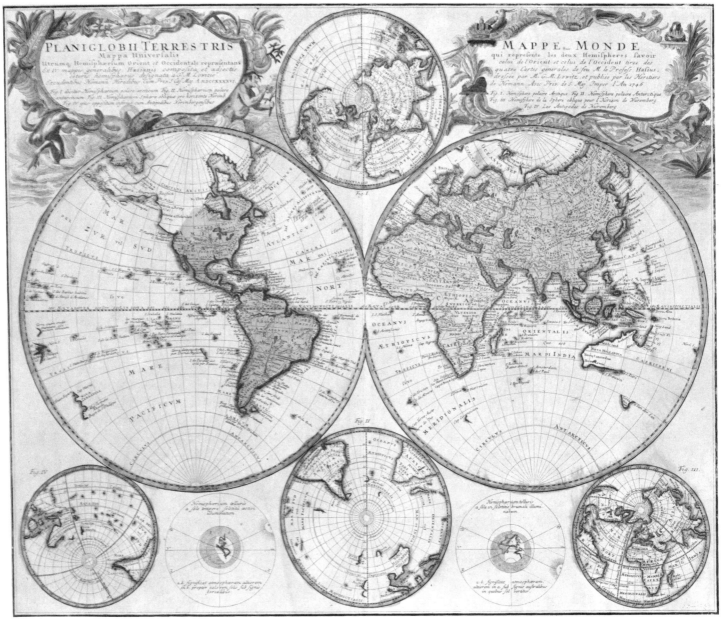

THE WORLD John Baptist Homann 1746   20½ × 17½ inches

impression. 1722—Thick paper with watermark about 3 inches in diameter of a horse within a circle. 1753 and 1772—These are usually on a good paper of smoother surface than 1722, and are very good black impressions, as they were re-engraved where necessary. There is also a small set of county maps, first issued in 1701 which are very attractive—some counties in particular being very charming. These are much scarcer than the large maps.

PHILIP CLUVERIUS. Maps of various parts of the world, including the Americas, and an attractive world in two hemispheres, were issued in the latter half of the seventeenth century, reissued in the beginning of the eighteenth. Each has a modest cartouche, but the general effect of each map is very pleasing.

SIR WILLIAM PETTY. Born at Romsey, Hampshire in 1623; studied on the continent, and became a mathematician and scientist of note. He also studied medicine and became Physician General to the army in Ireland, where other pursuits than medicine engaged his attention, for he undertook no less a task than the organising of a survey of the whole of the country, in which he was supported by Cromwell's Government. These maps were engraved in a crude and scratchy manner, often on paper sheets pasted together in irregular shapes and were published in 1685. Being the earliest county maps of Ireland, they are of great importance, and scarce. Another issue appeared in 1690, and a later reprinting, probably privately undertaken, came out sometime between 1850 and 1870. A miniature set was published in 1685 and in later issues to 1728. All these reissues are scarce.

EDWARD WELLS issued a set of maps of parts of the world at the end of the seventeenth century or about 1700 which are decorative, although quite without merit as maps. They are boldly engraved with few place names; they have a decorative cartouche and a dedication to the Duke of Gloucester, with his arms. The map of North America is of interest as it still shows California as an Island. There is also an interesting map of the British Plantations in America with insets of West Indian islands. The maps of the Ancient and the 'Modern' world, each in two hemispheres, are very decorative. Both have different scenes with figures at the base, with Oxford in the background, as the maps were printed there.

*JOHN SELLER. A mathematical instrument-maker to Charles I and James II and, until his death about 1700, the producer of many maps and sea charts covering all parts of the world. The items most likely to be seen are his fine 'English Pilot' or other sea charts which cover coasts in all parts of the world, and his set of miniature county maps issued in 1695 and reprinted in 1701. The cartouches were erased and a simple title substituted for the reissues from 1773 to the early nineteenth century, when they had a description of the county below the maps, and on the back.

*HERMAN MOLL came to England from his native Holland in the 1680's, engraving maps and selling both them and books, first in Blackfriars and later in Devereux Court, Strand. He probably worshipped in St. Clement Danes, as he died in the church on September 22nd 1732. His maps vary from miniatures to very large fine maps embellished with plans and pictures, and cover all parts of the world. There are some exceptionally large ones of Scotland, North America, The World, India, and East Indies to name but a few. His county maps are

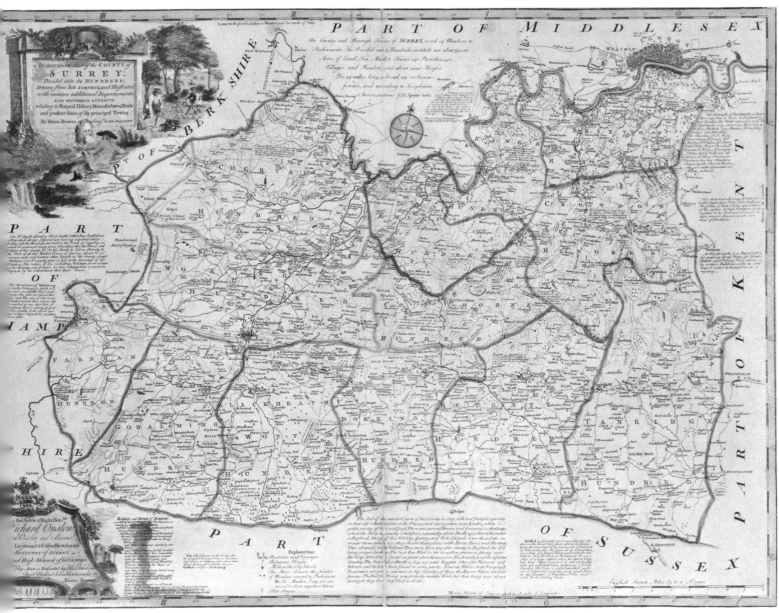

SURREY Emanuel Bowen, 1749–55 $27\frac{3}{4} \times 20\frac{5}{8}$ inches

of medium size and have an unusual feature in that they have representations of antiquities excavated in the county—coins, statues, Roman altars, or views of antiquities—Stonehenge, the Halifax Guillotine, the Eddystone Lighthouses etc. All his maps are engraved with a bold thick black line which is a peculiarity of his style.

JOHN SENEX also engraved some very fine maps, including a set of large ones of parts of the world. He flourished from 1700, probably beginning his business life as a bookseller. His premises were in Cornhill, and later at the sign of the Globe, Salisbury Court, Fleet Street. In 1719 he issued a small road book of strip maps after Ogilby, but without any decoration. In 1728 he produced a set of simple but practical sea charts in conjunction with Henry Wilson and John Harris. He died in 1740.

NICOLAS SANSON, born 1600 at Abbeville: died in 1667 at Paris. One of the greatest names in French map-making. His maps are always dignified and attractive, with an ornamental cartouche, often dated. The work was continued by his two sons, Guillaume and Adrien.

GUILLAUME DELISLE. Born in Paris in 1675, he produced a number of well-engraved and handsome maps, often with a decorative cartouche. His maps of various parts of the world are quite often come by, and are worth having. He died in 1726.

*EMANUEL BOWEN. A prolific engraver and map seller in Fleet Street, from about 1720 to 1767. It is difficult to realise the magnitude of the task involved in engraving a map, when every stroke of every letter of every place name has to be cut out of the copper with the burin, and Bowen appeared to make his county maps as complicated as possible, with the blank areas surrounding the county boundary filled with engraved text, describing the towns, their natural and manufactured products, situation and climate. These descriptions fill each county in the fine large series he made with Thomas Kitchin published in 1749-1755, in his medium sized maps of 1762 and his fine smaller maps of 1767, the year of his death. One of his productions was the beautiful 'Britannia Depicta' a work based upon Ogilby's road maps, but incorporating history, heraldry and cartography with its series of county maps, coats-of-arms, and notes filling every spare piece of the plate. There was, amongst many other productions, a series of small simple county maps, each with a rococo cartouche, and each bearing a date between 1759 and 1763. His son Thomas carried on the business and the tradition. He engraved many maps and reissued many of his father's, sometimes suitably altered to bring them up to date—the exuberant rococo cartouche would be erased, and the title placed within a simple circle or elipse. He lived in Clerkenwell and seems to have shared his Father's ill luck at the close of his life for he died in, of all places, the workhouse there in 1790. His father had ended his days without money and practically blind.

THOMAS BADESLADE and WILLIAM HENRY TOMS. In 1741-1742 a set of small maps of the English counties was published, engraved by Toms of Hatton Garden and later of Ludgate Hill, after Badeslade's designs. Although Badeslade was a surveyor, the maps are certainly not the result of much activity in this field. A column down the left-hand side gives a list of towns with Fairs and Market Days.

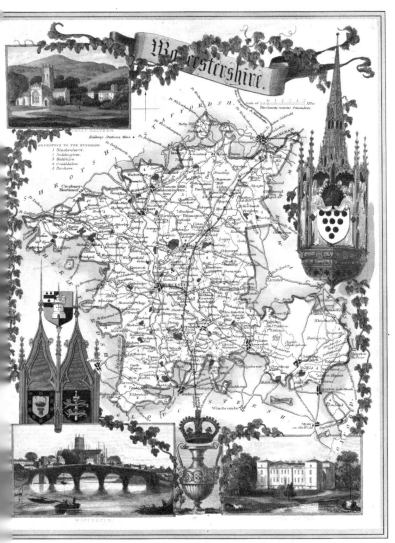

WORCESTERSHIRE Thomas Moule, 1784–1851
8 × 10½ inches

NEW SOUTH WALES John Tallis, 1850   9⅞ × 13½ inches

*JOHN ROCQUE, a Huguenot living in London, was a skilled engraver of many maps and plans between about 1734 and 1762. He changed his address several times and appears to have started at 'Ye Canister and Sugar Loaf' in Great Windmill Street, St. James, and moved to Hyde Park Corner, and then back to The Strand–Charing Cross area. He executed a set of county maps, mostly with hatching round each county boundary, sometimes embellishing the maps with a coat-of-arms or other feature. His far greater achievement was the magnificent survey of London he undertook, which was drawn upon a very large scale—and engraved by Pine from 1731 to the year of issue 1746.

THOMAS KITCHIN was another productive engraver of quality. In addition to his engraving he was a publisher, author of a small book of instruction on the various mediums of artistic expression, from water-colour to etching, and from oils to engraving; he also sold artists' materials of all types from his premises, at the Sign of the Star, which were situated at Holborn Hill. He engraved many maps, some of counties and others of parts of the world, and flourished between 1738 and 1776. He produced a very attractive set of quarto-sized county maps in 1764, each with a rococo cartouche.

THOMAS JEFFERYS, working in a not dissimilar style over the same period was also a publisher and an author. He engraved the English counties with Kitchin in a set of small maps first published in 1749; and maps of all parts of the world, concentrating a good deal on North America and the West Indies, of which parts some fine work was done. He died in 1771.

JOHN ELLIS. An engraver of maps, and much else, between about 1750–1796. He produced a set of county maps in 1766 which were obvious copies from the quarto maps of Thomas Kitchin, but instead of the rococo cartouche, a miniature scene is introduced, the title usually being shown upon a rock, around which a tree and some greenery usually flourishes. From a pocket-book of his in my possession it is possible to gain some idea of the extraordinary range of engraving undertaken by these skilled men. This book is for the year 1770, and the work executed includes: trade cards and bill headings for grocers, wine merchants, linen drapers, a gingerbread baker and other tradesmen; labels for Tincture for the Teeth, Gums and Toothache; visiting cards; titles to innumerable engraved portraits, a monogram on a watch case; promissory notes; lottery tickets; cheques; and even a name on a dog-collar, for which he received 1s. 0d.! A small tragedy is placed laconically amongst the business entries—
Sunday July 1st 1770 'Wife delivered of Son about quarter before ten in the morning'.
Thursday July 26th 1770 'Son Joseph died a little before eleven at night'.
Monday July 30th 1770 'Dues for burying the child—14s. 10d.

*GEORGE BICKHAM. Born 1684. He flourished at Covent Garden as an author and engraver from the beginning of the eighteenth century to about 1758. Only one of his works is of interest to us here, the set of strange bird's-eye view maps of the counties which was possibly published first in 1743 but certainly in 1754, with a slightly altered reissue in 1796. The maps show a view of the county seen from a hill upon which, filling the foreground, are classical ruins, the county being glimpsed between decaying pillars and broken archways. There are a few place names on each plate. They are attractive, scarce, and very unlike anything else.

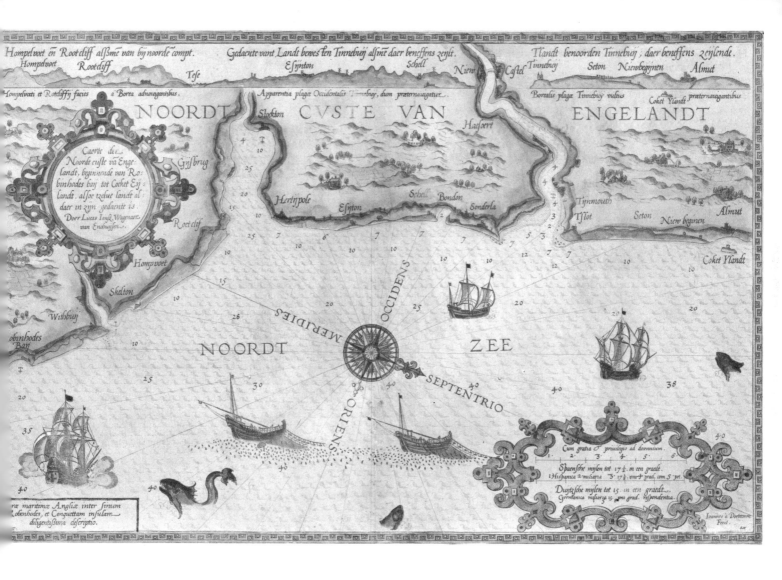

SEA CHART Lucas Waghenaer, 1584–8 20 × 13 inches

*ALEXANDER HOGG, a publisher in Paternoster Row, from about 1778. With Thomas Conder engraving the maps he published a set of counties in 1784–1786 and a number of maps of parts of the world during this period.

*JOHN CARY. One of the most prolific of all map-makers, and not only a superb engraver of fine accurate lettering on his maps, but the first to dispense with all decoration and really produce maps of utility, relying on their quality alone for any fine appearance they may have. He was born about 1754 and was certainly engraving by the late 1770's, his map-selling premises being in the Strand at No. 181, but these were burnt out on January 17th 1820, when he removed to St. James's Street. Amongst much else he made quarto-size county maps in 1793 and after, with many issues and newly engraved sets of maps of exactly the same appearance. There are also two folio sets of county maps which were issued in 1789 and 1805 respectively. These maps have interesting detail, with the roads and byroads shown. He died in August 1835.

*CHARLES SMITH produced a set of county maps in 1804 with later issues very similar in style to Cary. They are plain and undecorated, but of high quality and therefore attractive in their own way.

*CHRISTOPHER and JAMES GREENWOOD made maps of the English counties that are splendid productions, finely engraved with great detail— villages, hamlets and even some farms are shown by name, with roads and byroads. Each map has a large vignette of a famous building in the county, and a good deal of original hand colouring. The maps were made from their own surveys and are all dated between 1817 and 1834.

*THOMAS MOULE is best known for his set of maps of the English counties, the last of the antique decorative ones. Born in 1784, a writer on heraldry and antiquities, a bookseller, Inspector of Blind Letters at the General Post Office and latterly the holder of a post under the Lord Chamberlain which enabled him to live in Stable Yard, St. James's Palace, where he died in January 1851. His maps published in 1836, seen at their best, properly coloured and mounted, have a charm and decorative quality unlike that of any other map. Their delicacy, their wealth of exuberant foliage, shields, views, figures and 'gothick' ornamentation, have a charm that justifies the description of 'pretty'. He did not include any maps of Scotland, Wales or Ireland.

*PIGOT & CO., 1829. A well-produced set of maps of the English counties, each bearing a vignette view and giving considerable detail considering the scale. A miniature set, similar in style, but without the views, was published in 1835.

*REUBEN RAMBLE, 1845. In this year, under the somewhat unlikely name, a quaint little set of lithographed maps was published, covering all the English counties. The maps themselves are but a few inches square, but each is surrounded by a charming pictorial border showing rural scenes with farming in progress, scenes of specific parts of the county, and industrial scenes where appropriate; each suitable to the occupations, natural products, or industries of the county. They are scarce, and the reason is not far to seek—they were primarily printed for children, and undoubtedly became more and more tattered until finally thrown away.

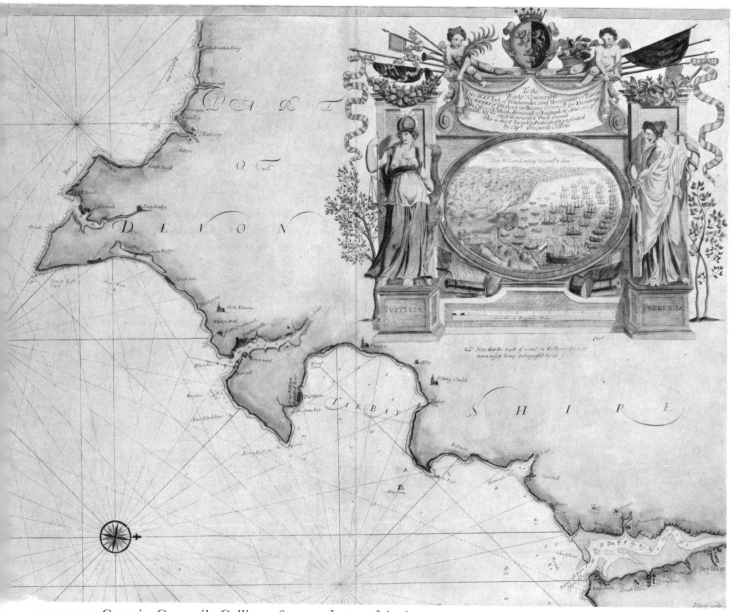

SEA CHART Captain Greenvile Collins, 1693   22⅜ × 17¾ inches

OTHER MAP-MAKERS IN BRIEF

TOMASO PORCACCHI, 1572. An interesting and decorative series of maps, mostly of islands. They are miniature in size, upon a sheet of text, but are very finely engraved with cartouches, and have the appearance of large maps reduced in size. There were several seventeenth century reissues.

H. SEILE—R. VAUGHAN. Although Vaughan engraved other maps these names are born by a series of four maps of the continents––Africa, Asia, Europe and America. They were first issued in 1652 bearing the name of Henry Seile. A later issue has the name of his widow—Ann Seile—this in turn is followed by the name of Robert Vaughan. The issues are all very similar in style and have a quaint decorative and antique appearance. The map of the Americas is particularly sought after, followed by that of Africa.

ALEXIS HUBERT JAILLOT and his family issued many superb maps from about 1680 to the mid-eighteenth century. Many are of large size with ornate cartouches in proportion.

MARCO VINCENZO CORONELLI produced a fine set of large, coarsely engraved maps in 1690–1697. The maps mostly have decoration, and where there is a cartouche or figure, it is always different—as are the maps—and often flamboyant. Scarce.

NICOLAS DE FER, 1693–1760. Although he made and issued a wide variety and considerable quantity of maps, his productions are not as frequently met with as one might expect. The maps are often attractive in appearance.

JOHN ADAIR. A rare set of six sea charts of parts of Scotland, printed in 1703. Also maps of the Lothians, and Perthshire. He died in 1722.

PIETER VAN DER AA, 1713–1714. A fine and most attractive series of maps, well-engraved, having detailed and beautifully executed cartouches, often with scenes in the background. He also produced a staggering work of several thousand maps and views, the Galerie Agréable du Monde, which is very rare, being limited to 100 copies.

MATTHEUS SEUTTER flourished 1720–1745. Very similar to Homann in style. There were two of the same name.

*J. COWLEY produced a number of simple but attractive little county maps, which were published in 1744.

R. W. SEALE engraved a number of maps in the mid-eighteenth century but is probably most noted for a set of different parts of the world, including a handsome one of North America, which were issued during the years 1744–1747.

ISAAC TIRION produced a well-engraved series of maps and plans in the eighteenth century, often without any ornamentation. Mostly c. 1730–1770.

JEAN BAPTISTE D'ANVILLE was responsible for a number of maps during the eighteenth century. He died in 1782, aged 85. His maps are seen less frequently than his name, which appears on a number of English and other atlases who used him as a source, or published his works in translation. From about 1740.

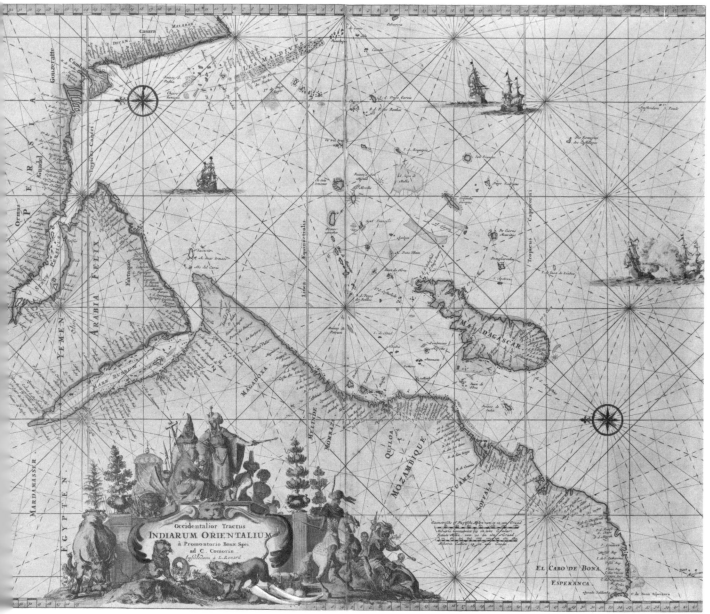

SEA CHART L. Renard, 1715   21¼ × 17½ inches

*SAMUEL SIMPSON, 1746. Produced a set of decorative little county maps, each embellished with one, sometimes two, coats-of-arms.

G. L. LEROUGE, flourished 1740–1780. Some attractive maps of parts of the world, specialising particularly in America, town plans, and plans of castles and fortifications.

*JOHN GIBSON engraved a number of maps, which include a set of small maps of the counties of England and Wales, first published in 1759, with later issues to about 1779. Also a delightful set of miniature maps of all parts of the world from 1758.

*G. ROLLOS. An engraver of maps, with a shop in Long Acre from which he sold prints and paintings. He produced some county maps, usually with a rococo cartouche, in the 1760's and 1770's.

WILLIAM FADEN took over Thomas Jeffery's business in 1771 and from then until well into the nineteenth century produced maps of considerable merit. The engraving is fine, the maps detailed. Faden's maps always repay close study.

A. JANVIER flourished in the 1770's; his maps are attractive and detailed, usually with a decorative cartouche.

G. A. RIZZI ZANNONI, 1762. Very beautiful maps—accurate and detailed; superbly engraved, with delightful cartouches.

J. HINTON. The publisher of the set of rather bleak little road maps, often with more than one road upon the sheet, taken from Ogilby, and published in his *Universal Magazine of Knowledge and Pleasure* between 1765 and 1773.

R. BONNE produced two sets of maps and charts, c. 1760–1788 mostly without decoration, and relatively undistinguished, but they are still early enough to be of interest. Maps usually bear his name as M. Bonne.

L. C. DESNOS. A Frenchman who introduced a series of maps of medium size, well-engraved, some within a most attractive ornamental rococo border or frame, mostly between 1760 and 1790.

TAYLOR & SKINNER, 1776. Maps of roads in Scotland not often found in single sheets as different maps were printed upon both sides of the paper.

J. M. ARMSTRONG. Set of small maps of Scottish counties, 1777–1794.

CONRAD LOTTER. Produced maps from early in the eighteenth century to about 1778, publishing Seutter maps, and being published by the house of Homann.

ANTONIO ZATTA, 1779–1785. Attractive maps, which include groups of English counties. Sometimes the engraving has a strange scratchy appearance, but the maps, and more particularly the cartouches, have bright colour applied crudely but effectively.

ROBERT de VAUGONDY. A name frequently to be met with, as not only are there many maps by the two de Vaugondy's, but a number of maps issued later in this country and elsewhere acknowledged the name as their source. The maps have many place names, are more accurate than most of their predecessors, and are embellished with a cartouche. The elder Robert is often given on maps as Le Sieur Robert. They covered the years 1740–1780 approximately.

TOWN PLAN Sebastian Munster, 1545 $13\frac{3}{4} \times 10\frac{1}{2}$ inches

ROBERT SAYER. A map and book publisher in Fleet Street, where he also sold prints, from the middle to the end of the eighteenth century. He republished many maps and atlases, by Jefferys, Bowen, Kitchin, and Ellis. The latter part of his business career was in partnership with John Bennett. This continued until 1784 when Sayer again carried on alone until about 1794 when Laurie & Whittle took over the business and continued to publish some very fine maps, although at this period they were not very decorative.

JOHN BAPTIST HOMANN and his heirs produced very many maps throughout the eighteenth century. Each map has a large, sometimes very large, cartouche with figures which is very effective though heavy in style. See remarks for Lotter.

JOHN LUFFMAN, 1803–1806. A quaint but well-engraved set of tiny county maps of England and Wales, each within a 2⅜-inch circle, with text below. Scarce. Also an interesting series of small maps and plans, all coloured, with his imprint and date upon each.

*J. ROPER was the engraver of a set of maps of English and Welsh counties after G. Cole which are variously dated from 1805 to 1810 in which year they were published. The work is of a very high standard, and the issues of this period are attractive in appearance, often having early colouring on the map face and border. With the county maps a number of town plans was included, again finely executed. A later lithographed version printed in 1858 is very poor in quality.

J. WALLIS, 1810 and H. MILLER, 1820. Both issued a number of neat little lithographic maps of English counties and other parts, of miniature size. They are not dissimilar in appearance.

LANGLEY & BELCH, 1817–1820. An attractive set of maps of English and Welsh counties, each with a view of a county or other town, a famous building or a scene.

HENRY TEESDALE. Well engraved maps of counties in two versions; the larger size (1829) were reprints of an 1816 series by R. Rowe. There is also a travelling version of small size (1830). Maps of all parts of the world of about the same period. The maps usually have the original wash colouring.

Lt. ROBT. K. DAWSON. A very complete series of plans of boroughs and cities in England and Wales issued to show the revised boundaries after the passing of the Boundaries Act of 1832, and printed in that year. Not decorative in any way, but they often show towns seldom singled out in this way.

*ARCHIBALD FULLARTON & CO., of Glasgow published some maps of counties and various parts of the world that are worthy of notice. The set of English counties dating from 1833 to 1836 each have a vignette of some well-known building or town in the county and are well-engraved. The maps of parts of the world—(not all parts; the atlas was a peculiar production where accurate maps entirely without ornament alternated with lithographed maps, each surrounded by a number of scenes of natives, towns and animals) was issued in 1860. The decorative maps are usually of the more out-of-the-way parts of the world, whilst the large and populous countries are shown upon the plain maps.

SIDNEY HALL. County maps (1833 to the middle of the century); and maps of parts of the world, c. 1840–1857.

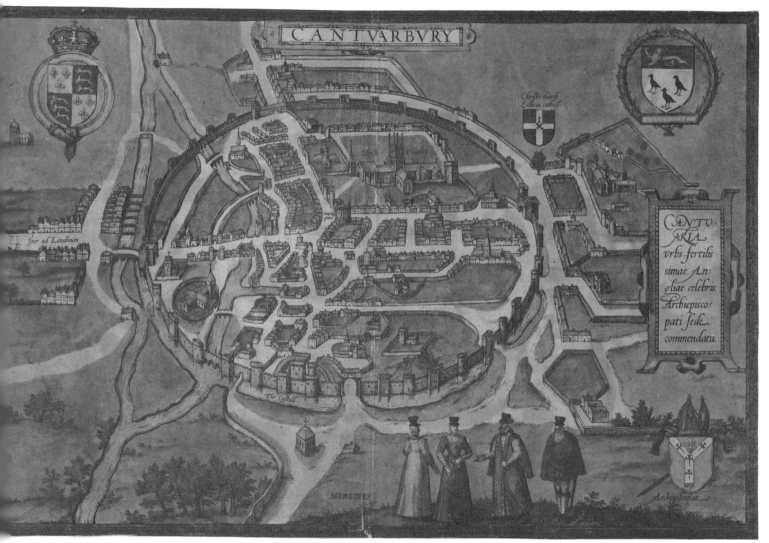

TOWN PLAN G. Braun and R. Hogenburg, 1564–73   17 × 11⅜ inches

JOHN TALLIS, 1850. A fine and ornate series of maps of all parts of the world, each with a decorative border and embellished with scenes, natives and animals. Tallis also published some very good town plans which, although rather less ornate, still have some views and a border.

SEA CHARTS

Many fine and decorative charts were produced by map makers of fame and note, including Blaeu, Jefferys, de Wit, and others, but other famous names are noted more for their nautical charts than their other productions, if any. Some of these are listed below.

The basic difference between a chart and a map is that a map is centred on the land, whereas the chart is a map of the sea; the chart, therefore, will show coastlines, with rocks, cliffs, anchorages, prominent buildings, hills, or other features near the coast, but no inland detail. The earlier examples are handsomely embellished with cartouches of intricate design to which some add ships and sea monsters. A frequent feature at all periods was a view of the land as seen from the sea, showing the shape of the natural features and position of sea-marks.

The dates given refer to the approximate span of dates of their production with subsequent re-issues.

LUCAS JANSZ WAGHENAER produced some magnificently decorative sea-charts published from 1584–1588 to the turn of the century. Those of the East and South coasts of the British Isles are the earliest printed charts of our coasts, and one would be a prize in any collection. The British place names have been engraved in their old Dutch form which does not always make for speedy legibility. Each chart is embellished with car-touches, monsters, ships and other features which appear on some to take precedence over any nautical information provided, to the undoubted detriment of navigation but in its Elizabethan exuberance, very much to our taste today.

SIR ROBERT DUDLEY was an innovator of note, as he produced the first set of charts based on Mercator's projection. He had sailed the world before settling in Florence, and his fine set of charts was published in 1646, to be followed in 1661 by another edition. The charts are rare, but the chance of obtaining one occurs from time to time. They are plain in style, but of unusual interest.

JACQUES NICOLAS BELLIN, born 1703 in Paris, dying at Versailles at the age of 69, was the maker of some very fine large charts, mostly embellished with rococo cartouches. There is also a smaller set of attractive charts. The larger works mostly bear the stamp of the Office of French Marine, with which Bellin was connected.

H. DONCKER, 1659–1666: P. GOOS, 1660–1676: J. Van Keulen, 1690–1726: R. & J. Ottens, 1690–1756 and L. Renard, 1715–1745 amongst others in the Low Countries, produced fine sea charts with decorative cartouches, often with figures, which are very similar in style, being, in fact, reprinted by other publishers, with their own imprint.

ROMAIN DE HOOGE, 1693–1694. A fine set of large charts of somewhat different style from those above.

CAPTAIN GREENVILE COLLINS, 1693–1785 compiled an original survey of the coasts of the British Isles. These important charts are as interesting as they are attractive, each being embellished

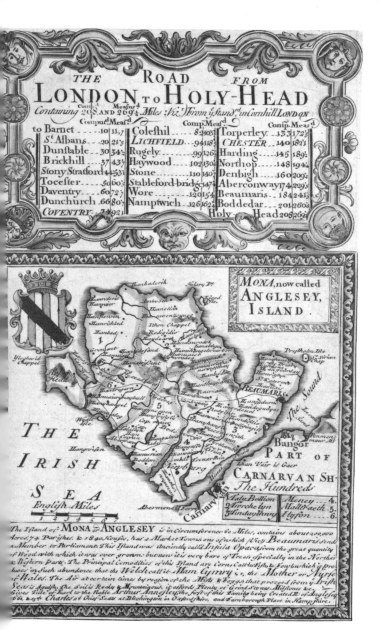

ANGLESEY Emanuel Bowen, 1720 $4\frac{1}{2} \times 7\frac{1}{4}$ inches

OXFORDSHIRE Robert Morden, 1701 $6\frac{1}{4} \times 8\frac{1}{8}$ inches

with a decorative cartouche. When well coloured, which is all too seldom, they present a handsome appearance. There are general charts in the series— the East Coast, St. George's Channel, the Coast of Wales, the Channel and the East Coast of Scotland for example, but there are more local ones that are especially interesting, such as Harwich (dedicated to Samuel Pepys), Rye; Aberdeen; Fowey; Torbay; Dartmouth; Holyhead, and many others. First published in 1693, they were often reprinted during the eighteenth century. Collins was a brother of Trinity House and commenced his seven-year survey in 1681.

JOHN SELLER not only executed maps, but fathered a tremendous flood of fine and interesting charts covering all parts of the world, from 1671 to the beginning of the eighteenth century. The later issues were published by Mount & Page, or another of Mount's partners—Thornton or Davidson.

JOHN SENEX, 1728. A set of very plain charts, sometimes several to a sheet, was issued, engraved by John Senex and published in conjunction with John Harris and Henry Wilson.

JOHN ADAIR, 1703. A scarce set of only seven charts of parts of Scotland, most delicately engraved, of very considerable interest and variety.

Other Names that may be met with include Arnold Colom 1656–1669; J. Van Loon 1661–1668; William Heather 1796–1808 (many of these were of very small size); T. Jacobsz 1648—early eighteenth century; Thomas Jefferys 1760–1770's includes a very detailed and efficient set relating to the West Indies and America; Bougard 1694–1801 and De Wit, 1660–1675. Blaeu issued a set of quite small charts from 1608 for a number of years.

TOWN PLANS

SEBASTIAN MUNSTER, 1540. A number of his woodcut maps and town views, usually of the bird's-eye view type, were issued from about this date. They are of very great interest, with each house realistically shown, and the immediate environs of the town with bridges, boats on the rivers; the gallows; and fingers shown in detail.

G. BRAUN & R. HOGENBURG of Cologne worked on a set of bird's-eye views of cities of the world which were published from 1564 until 1620. Each is a fine and beautiful production usually having a title within a cartouche in the sky or to one side at the base, often with some figures standing in the foreground, apparently upon the side of a hill above the city, whilst the viewer is a little higher up the slope. The cities depicted in the British Isles were—London; Edinburgh; Bristol; Cambridge; Canterbury; Exeter; Oxford; Norwich; Chester; York and Dublin.

RUTGER HERMANN, 1661. A very attractive series of miniature plans covering a very wide range of British towns and cities.

J. ANDREWS, 1771. A series of well executed plans on a small scale of towns and cities in all parts of the world. Each has a small but brave attempt at a decorative cartouche.

JOHN ROCQUE made a few large-scale plans each in several sheets, including Bristol (1750) Dublin (1756) and a magnificent London (1746) in twenty-four sheets which can sometimes be purchased separately. A very attractive little set of plans, almost always with original colouring was published about 1769, of eighteen towns in the

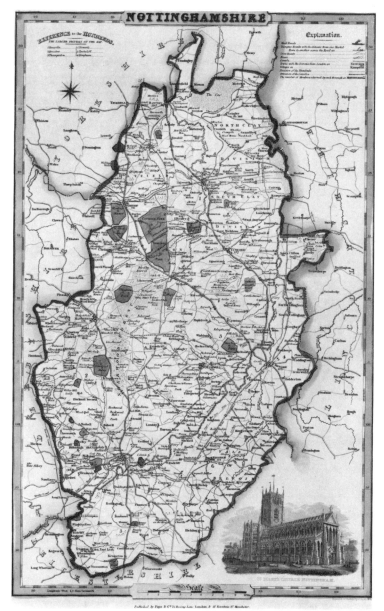

WILTSHIRE Herman Moll, 1724 $7\frac{1}{2} \times 12\frac{1}{2}$ inches   NOTTINGHAMSHIRE Pigot & Co, 1831 $8\frac{3}{4} \times 14$ inches

British Isles, including Aberdeen, Bristol, London, Edinburgh, Shrewsbury, Boston, Exeter, Chichester etc.

G. COLE & J. ROPER, 1805–1809. A very nicely engraved set of plans of many county and other towns in England. Each plan has a view, or coat-of-arms, or both. Although the scale is small, the detail is considerable.

THOMAS MOULE, 1836. Only three plans of English cities were made, but they are so delightful that a place must be made for them here; Oxford and Cambridge each embellished with the arms of the colleges, and a view; and Boston, Lincs. Moule also did maps of the environs of Bath–Bristol area; Plymouth; Portsmouth; and an attractive one of the environs of London which is scarcer, as it did not appear with the later issues of his maps.

BALDWIN & CRADOCK, 1833–1850. A series of maps and plans all finely and accurately executed. The plans cover many of the principal cities of the world, including New York, Boston and Philadelphia. They are still relatively low in price. They were first published by the Society for the Diffusion of Useful Knowledge.

JOHN TALLIS, 1850. An accurate and attractive series, not by any means as common as the Tallis maps. Each has a decorative border and a number of vignettes of scenes or buildings in the city. They cover a number of cities in the British Isles and in other parts of the world, including New York and Boston.

From the sixteenth century to the nineteenth century many fine large plans were issued, covering practically every city in the world. They are always worth having, and if one is acquainted with the town shown, are amongst the most interesting of all maps to study.

LARGE-SCALE MAPS
Also of extreme interest when closely examined are the large-scale surveys. There have been such surveys of one sort or another since the earliest days of printed maps, and fine and rare examples exist in many parts of the world of such maps of the sixteenth and seventeenth centuries. The real incentive to produce a large-scale map, however, was given by the Royal Society of Arts, founded in 1754, who offered a series of monetary awards for maps of one or two inches to the mile based on original surveys. As a result, there are maps of nearly all the English counties which are made to these scales, each in a number of sheets, until the 1820's. From this time C. & J. Greenwood began their own magnificent series, mostly on a scale of one inch to the mile, and all dated between 1817 and 1830. They were published at a time when the Ordnance Survey was in full swing—having been founded by the Duke of Richmond in 1791, and in progress until completed in 1867—but they differ in style, and the Greenwood maps even show such detail as gallows and toll gates.

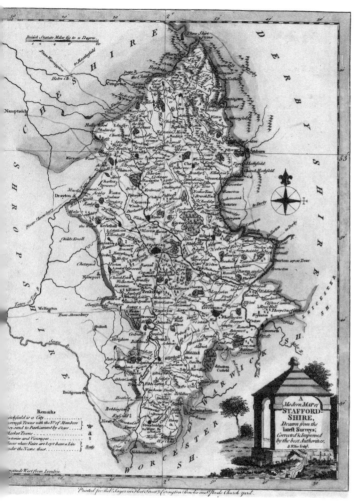

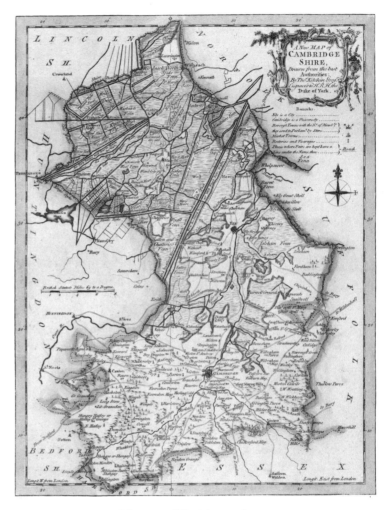

STAFFORDSHIRE John Ellis, 1766 $7\frac{1}{2}$ × 10 inches   CAMBRIDGESHIRE Thomas Kitchin $7\frac{5}{8}$ × 10 inches

BIBLIOGRAPHY

Maps and Map-Makers, R. V. Tooley, Batsford. The best book on the subject for the general reader. Invaluable. 1961.
How to Identify Old Maps and Globes by Raymond Lister. Bell, 1965. 70s. od. Much useful information.
Decorative Printed Maps of the Fifteenth to Eighteenth Centuries, R. A. Skelton. Good plates. 1958.

The Map Collectors Circle issues finely-produced, authoritative publications to subscribers upon a variety of aspects of early maps, including the issue of a new '*Chubb*' '*County Atlases of the British Isles 1579–1850*,' by R. A. Skelton, of the Map Room, British Museum. The standard reference for the county maps.

Subscription £5 5s. od. per annum. Address: Durrant House, Chiswell Street, London, E.C.1.

INDEX

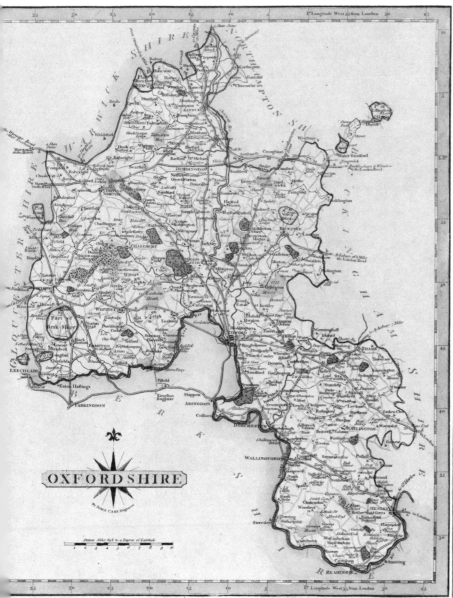

WORCESTERSHIRE Pieter Van Den Keere,
1599–1610 $4\frac{3}{4} \times 3\frac{3}{8}$ inches

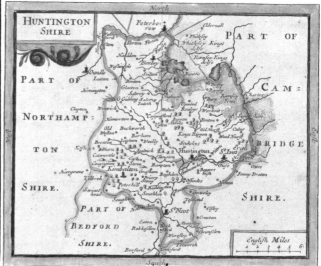

OXFORDSHIRE John Cary, 1793 $8\frac{1}{4} \times 10\frac{1}{4}$ inches

HUNTINGDONSHIRE John Seller, 1695 $5\frac{3}{4} \times 4\frac{3}{4}$ inches

HEREFORDSHIRE George Bickham, 1743–54
5¾ × 9 inches

DERBYSHIRE Emanuel Bowen, 1767
8¾ × 12¾ inches